The Travel

Hávamál

The sayings of the

High One

Translations of Verses by Olive Bray.

CW01335790

Table of Contents

The Hávamál

Part 1 - Counsels (1-79)

1. At every door-way,
before one enters,
one should spy round,
one should pry round
for uncertain is the witting
that there be no foeman sitting,
within, before one on the floor

2. Hail to the giver!
A guest has come;
Where shall the stranger sit?
Swift shall he be who,
with swords shall try
The proof of his might to make.

3. He has need of fire,
who now is come,
numbed with cold to the knee;
food and clothing
the wanderer craves
who has fared over the rimy fell.

4. He craves for water,
who comes for refreshment,
drying and friendly bidding,
marks of good will,
fair fame if it is won,
and welcome once and again.

5. He has need of his wits
who wanders wide,
anything simple
will serve at home;
but a gazing-stock
is the fool who sits
mid the wise,
and nothing knows.

6. Let no man glory
in the greatness of his mind,
but rather keep watch
over his wits.
Cautious and silent
let him enter a dwelling;
to the heedful
comes seldom harm,
for none can find
a more faithful friend
than the wealth of mother wit.

7. Let the wary stranger
who seeks refreshment
keep silent
with sharpened hearing
with his ears let him listen,
and look with his eyes;
thus each wise man
spies out the way.

8. Happy is he who wins for himself
fair fame and kindly words;
but uneasy is that
which a man owns
while it lies in another's breast.

9. Happy is he who has in himself
praise and wisdom in life;
for often does a man ill counsel get
when it is born in another's breast.

10. A better burden can no man bear
on the way than his mother wit;
it is the refuge of the poor,
and richer it seems
than wealth in a world untried.

11. A better burden can no man bear
on the way than his mother wit:
and no worse provision
can he carry with him
than too deep a draught of ale.

12. Less good than they say
for the sons of men
is the drinking often of ale:
for the more they drink,
the less can they think
and keep a watch over their wits.

13. A bird of unmindfulness
Flutters over ale feasts,
wiling away men's wits:
with the feathers of that fowl
I was fettered once
in the garths of Gunnlos below.

14. Drunk was I then,
I was over drunk
in that crafty Jotun's court.
But best is an ale feast
when man is able
to call back his wits at once.

15. Silent and thoughtful
and bold in strife
the prince's bairn should be.
Joyous and generous
let each man show him
till he shall suffer death.

16.A coward believes
he will ever live
if he keep him safe from strife:
but old age leaves him
not long in peace
though spears may spare his life.

17.A fool will gape
when he goes to a friend,
and mumble only, or mope;
but pass him the ale cup
and all in a moment
the mind of that man is shown.

18. He knows alone
who has wandered wide,
and far has fared on the way,
what manner of mind
a man owns
who is wise of head and heart.

19. Keep not the mead cup
but drink your measure;
speak needful words or none:
none shall upbraid you
for lack of breeding
if soon you seek'st your rest.

20. A greedy man,
if he be not mindful,
eats to his own life's hurt:
often the belly of the fool
will bring him to scorn
when he seeks
the circle of the wise.

21. Herds know the hour
of their going home
and turn them again
from the grass;
but never is found a foolish man
who knows the measure of his maw.

22. The miserable man
and evil minded
makes of all things mockery,
and knows not
that which he best should know,
that he is not free from faults.

23. The unwise man
is awake all night,
and ponders everything over;
when morning comes
he is weary in mind,
and all is a burden as ever.

24. The unwise man
weens all who smile
and flatter him are his friends,
nor notes how often
they speak him ill
when he sits
in the circle of the wise.

25. The unwise man
weens all who smile
and flatter him are his friends;
but when he shall come into court
he shall find
there are few to defend his cause.

26. The unwise man
thinks all to know
while he sits in a sheltered nook;
but he knows not one thing,
what he shall answer,
if men shall put him to proof.

27. For the unwise man
it is best to be mute
when he come amid the crowd,
for none is aware of his lack of wit
if he wastes not too many words;
for he who lacks wit
shall never learn
though his words
flow never so fast.

28. Wise he is deemed
who can question well,
and also answer back:
the sons of men
can no secret make
of the ridings told in their midst.

29. Too many unstable words
are spoken by him
who never holds his peace;
the hasty tongue
sings its own mishap
if it be not bridled in.

30. Let no man be held
as a laughing-stock,
though he is a guest for a meal
wise enough seem many
while they sit dry-skinned
and are not put to proof.

31. A guest thinks him witty
who mocks at a guest
and runs from his wrath away;
but none can be sure
who jests at a meal
that he makes not fun among foes.

32. Often, though their hearts
lean towards one another,
friends are divided at table;
ever the source of strife it will be,
that guest will anger guest.

33. A man should take
always his meals betimes
unless he visit a friend,
or he sits and mopes,
and half famished seems,
and can ask or answer nothing.

34. Long is the round
to a false friend leading,
even if he dwell on the way:
but though far off fared,
to a faithful friend
straight are the roads and short.

35. A guest must depart
again on his way,
nor stay in the same place ever;
if he bide too long
on another's bench
the loved one soon becomes loathed.

36. One's own house is best,
though small it may be;
each man is master at home;
though he have but two goats
and a bark-thatched hut
it is better than craving a boon.

37. One's own house is best,
though small it may be,
each man is master at home;
with a bleeding heart
will he beg, who must,
his meat at every meal.

38. Let a man never stir
on his road a step
without his weapons of war;
for unsure is the knowing
when need shall arise
of a spear on the way without.

39. Let no man stint him
and suffer need
of the wealth he has won in life;
often is saved for a foe
what was meant for a friend,
and much goes worse
than one weens.

40. Found none so noble
or free with his food,
who was not gladdened
with a gift,
nor one who gave
of his gifts such store
but he loved reward,
could he win it.

41. With raiment and arms
shall friends gladden each other,
so has one proved oneself;
for friends last longest,
if fate be fair
who give and give again.

42. To his friend
a man should bear him as friend,
and gift for gift betow,
laughter for laughter
let him exchange,
but leasing pay for a lie.

43. To his friend
a man should bear him as friend,
to him and a friend of his;
but let him beware
that he be not the friend
of one who is friend to his foe.

44. Have you got a friend
that you trust well,
from whom you crave good?
Share your mind with him,
gifts exchange with him,
fare to find him often.

45. But have you one
whom you trust ill
yet from whom you crave good?
You shall speak him fair,
but falsely think,
and leasing pay for a lie.

46. Yet further of him
whom you trusted ill,
and whose mind
thou dost misdoubt;
though shall laugh with him
but withhold your thought,
for gift with like gift
should be paid.

47. Young was I once,
I walked alone,
and bewildered
seemed in the way;
then I found me another
and rich I thought me,
for man is the joy of man.

48. Most blest is he
who lives free and bold
and nurses never a grief,
for the fearful man
is dismayed by anything,
and the mean one
mourns over giving.

49. My garments once
I gave in the field
to two land-marks made as men;
heroes they seemed
when once they were clothed;
it is the naked who suffer shame!

50. The pine tree wastes
which is perched on the hill,
nor bark nor needles shelter it;
such is the man that no one loves;
what should he live longer for?

51. Fiercer than fire among ill friends
for five days love will burn;
but anon it is quenched,
when the sixth day comes,
and all friendship soon is spoiled.

52. Not great things alone
must one give to another,
praise often is earned for nothing;
with half a loaf and a tilted bowl
I have found me many a friend.

53. Little the sand if little the seas,
little are minds of men,
for never in the world
were all equally wise,
it is shared by the fools
and the sage.

54. Wise in measure let each man be;
but let him not wax too wise;
for never the happiest
of men, is he who knows
much of many things.

55. Wise in measure
should each man be;
but let him not wax too wise;
seldom a heart will sing with joy
if the owner be all too wise.

56. Wise in measure
should each man be,
but never let him wax too wise:
who does not look forward
to learn his fate
unburdened heart will bear.

57. Brand kindles from brand
till it be burned,
spark is kindled from spark,
man unfold him
by speech with man,
but grows over secret
through silence.

58. He must rise betimes
who fain of another
or life or wealth would win;
scarce falls the prey
to sleeping wolves,
or to slumberers victory in strife.

59. He must rise betimes
who has few to serve him,
and see to his work himself;
who sleeps at morning
is hindered much,
to the keen is wealth half-won.

60. Of dry logs saved
and roof-bark stored
a man can know the measure,
of fire-wood too
which should last him out
quarter and half years to come.

61. Fed and washed
should one ride to court
though in garments
none too new;
you shall not shame you
for shoes or breeks,
nor yet for a sorry steed.

62. Each man who is wise
and would wise be called
must ask and answer aright.
Let one know your secret,
but never a second, -
if three a thousand shall know.

63. As the eagle who comes
to the ocean shore,
Sniffs and hangs her head,
Dumfounded is he
who finds at the Thing
No supporters to plead his case.

64. A wise counseled man
will be mild in bearing
and use his might in measure,
lest when he come
his fierce foes among
he find others fiercer than he.

65. *Each man should be watchful*
and wary in speech,
and slow to put faith in a
*friend.**
For the words
which one to another speaks
he may wind reward of ill.

* *The first three lines are a later interpolation*

66. At many a feast I was far too late,
and much too soon at some;
drunk was the ale
or yet unserved:
never hits he the joint
who is hated.

67. Here and there to a home
I had haply been asked
had I needed no meat
at my meals,
or were two hams left hanging
in the house of that friend
where I had partaken of one.

68. Most dear is fire
to the sons of men,
most sweet the sight of the sun;
good is health
if one can but keep it,
and to live a life without shame.

69. Not reft of all is he who is ill,
for some are blest in their bairns,
some in their kin
and some in their wealth,
and some in working well.

70. More blest are the living
than the lifeless,
it is the living
who come by the cow;
I saw the hearth-fire burn
in the rich man's hall
and himself
lying dead at the door

71. The lame can ride rose,
the handless drive cattle,
the deaf one can fight and prevail,
it is happier for the blind
than for him on the bale-fire,
but no man has care for a corpse.

72. Best have a son
though he be late born
and before him the father be dead:
seldom are stones
raised on the wayside
save by kinsmen to kinsmen.

73. Two are hosts against one,
the tongue is the head's bane,
'neath a rough hide
a hand may be hid.

74. He is glad at night fall
who knows of his lodging,
short is the ship's berth,
and changeful the autumn night,
much veers the wind
before the fifth day
and blows round
yet more in a month.

75. He who learns nothing
will never know
how one is the fool of another,
for if one be rich another is poor
and for that should bear no blame.

76. Cattle die and kinsmen die,
yourself too soon must die,
but one thing
will never die, I think
– the doom on each one dead.

77. Cattle die and kinsmen die,
yourself too soon must die,
but one thing never,
I think, will die, -
fair fame of one who has earned.

78. Full-stocked folds
had the Fatling's sons,
who bear now a beggar's staff:
brief is wealth,
as the winking of an eye,
most faithless ever of friends.

79. If haply a fool
should find for himself
wealth or a woman's love,
pride waxes in him
but wisdom never
and onward he fares in his folly.

The Hávamál

Part 2a - Proverbs (80 - 90)

80. All will prove true
that you ask of runes –
those that are come from the gods,
which the high Powers wrought,
and which Odin painted:
then silence is surely best.

81. Praise day at even,
a wife when dead,
a weapon when tried,
a maid when married,
ice when it is crossed,
and ale when it is drunk.

82. Hew wood in wind,
sail the seas in a breeze,
woo a maid in the dark,
- for day's eyes are many, -
work a ship for its gliding,
a shield for its shelter,
a sword for its striking,
a maid for her kiss;

83. Drink ale by the fire,
but slide on the ice;
buy a steed when it is lanky,
a sword when it is rusty;
feed your horse neath a roof,
and your hound in the yard.

84. The speech of a maiden
should no man trust
nor the words
which a woman says;
for their hearts were shaped
on a whirling wheel
and falsehood
fixed in their breasts.

85. Breaking bow,
or flaring flame,
ravening wolf,
or croaking raven,
routing swine,
or rootless tree,
waxing wave,
or seething cauldron,

86. Flying arrows,
or falling billow,
ice of a night time,
coiling adder,
woman's bed-talk,
or broken blade,
play of bears
or a prince's child,

87. Sickly calf
or self-willed thrall,
witch's flattery,
new-slain foe,

88. Let none put faith
in the first sown fruit
nor yet in his son too soon;
whim rules the child,
and weather the field,
each is open to chance.

89. Brother's slayer,
though seen on the highway,
half burned house,
or horse too swift –
be never so trustful
as these to trust.

90. Like the love of women
whose thoughts are lies
is the driving un-roughshod
over slippery ice
of a two year old,
ill-tamed and gay;
or in a wild wind steering
a helmless ship,
or the lame catching reindeer
in the rime-thawed fell.

The Hávamál

Part 2b - Ensamples of Óðinn (91-110)

91. Now plainly I speak,
since both I have seen;
unfaithful is man to maid;
we speak them fairest
when thoughts are falsest
and wile the wisest of hearts.

92. Let him speak soft words
and offer wealth
who longs for a woman's love,
praise the shape
of the shining maid –
he wins who thus woos.

93. Never a whit
should one blame another
whom love
has brought into bonds:
often a witching form
will fetch the wise
which does not hold
the heart of fools.

94. Never a whit
should one blame another
for a folly which many befalls;
the might of love
makes sons of men into fools
who once were wise.

95. The mind knows alone
what is nearest the heart
and sees where the soul is turned:
no sickness seems to the wise so sore
as in nothing to know content.

96. This once I felt when I sat
Without in the reeds,
and looked for my love;
body and soul of me
was that sweet maiden
yet never I won her as wife.

97. Billing's daughter
I found on her bed,
fairer than sunlight sleeping,
and the sweets of lordship
seemed to me nothing,
save I lived with that lovely form.

98. "Yet nearer evening
come you, Óðinn,
if you will woo a maiden:
all were undone
save two knew alone
such a secret deed of shame."

99. So away I turned
from my wise intent,
and deemed my joy assured,
for all her liking and all her love
I thought that I yet should win.

100. When I came before long
the war troop bold
were watching and waking all:
with burning brands
and torches borne
they showed me
my sorrowful way.

101. Yet nearer morning
I went, once more, -
the housefolk slept in the hall,
but soon I found a barking dog
tied fast to that fair maid's couch.

102. Many a sweet maid
when one knows her mind
is fickle found towards men:
I proved it well
when that prudent lass
I sought to lead astray:
shrewd maid,
she sought me with every insult
and I won therewith no wife.

103. In your home be joyous
and generous to guests
discreet shall you be
in your bearing,
mindful and talkative,
would you gain wisdom,
often making me mention of good.
He is "Simpleton" named
who has nothing to say,
for such is the fashion of fools.

104. I sought that old Jotun,
now safe am I back,
little served my silence there;
but whispering
many soft speeches
I won my desire
in Suttung's halls.

105. It was Gunnlod who gave me
on a golden throne
a draught of the glorious mead,
but with poor reward
did I pay her back
for her true and troubled heart.

106. I bored me a road there
with Rati's tusk
and made room to pass
through the rock;
while the ways of the Jotuns
stretched over and under,
I dared my life for a draught.

107. In a wily disguise
I worked my will;
little is lacking to the wise,
for the Soul-stirrer now,
sweet Mead of Song,
is brought to men's earthly abode.

108. I misdoubt me
if ever again I had come
from the realms of the Jotun race,
had I not served me of Gunnlod,
sweet woman,
her whom I held in mine arms.

109. Came forth, next day,
the dread Frost Giants,
and entered the High One's Hall:
they asked – was the Baleworker
back mid the Powers,
or had Suttung slain him below?

110. A ring-oath Óðinn
I trow had taken –
how shall one trust his troth?
It was he who stole
the mead from Suttung,
and Gunnlod caused to weep.

The Hávamál

Part 3 - Lay of Loddfáfnir (111-137)

111. It is time to speak
from the Sage's Seat;
hard by the Well of Weird
I saw and was silent,
I saw and pondered,
I listened to the speech of men.

Of runes they spoke,
and the reading of runes
was little withheld from their lips:
at the High One's hall,
in the High One's hall,
I thus heard the High One say:

112. I counsel you, Stray-Singer,
accept my counsels,
they will be your boon
if you obey them,
they will work your weal
if you win them:
rise never at night time,
except you are spying
or seekest a spot without.

113. I counsel you, Stray-Singer,
accept my counsels,
they will be your boon
if you obey them,
they will work your weal
if you win them:
you shall never sleep
in the arms of a sorceress,
lest she should lock your limbs;

114. So shall she charm
that you shall not heed
the council, or words of the king,
nor care for your food,
or the joys of mankind,
but fall into sorrowful sleep.

115. I counsel you, Stray-Singer,
accept my counsels,
they will be your boon
if you obey them,
they will work your weal
if you win them:
seek not ever to draw to yourself
in love-whispering
another's wife.

116. I counsel you, Stray-Singer,
accept my counsels,
they will be your boon
if you obey them,
they will work your weal
if you win them:
should you long to fare
over fell and firth
provide you well with food.

117. I counsel you, Stray-Singer,
accept my counsels,
they will be your boon
if you obey them,
they will work your weal
if you win them:
tell not ever an evil man
if misfortunes you befall,
from such ill friend
you need never seek
return for your trustful mind.

118. Wounded to death,
have I seen a man
by the words of an evil woman;
a lying tongue
had bereft him of life,
and all without reason of right.

119. I counsel you, Stray-Singer,
accept my counsels,
they will be your boon
if you obey them,
they will work your weal
if you win them:
have you a friend
whom you trustest well,
fare you to find him often;
for with brushwood grows
and with grasses high
the path where no foot passes.

120. I counsel you, Stray-Singer,
accept my counsels,
they will be your boon
if you obey them,
they will work your weal
if you win them:
in sweet converse
call the righteous
to your side,
learn a healing song
while you live.

121. I counsel you, Stray-Singer,
accept my counsels,
they will be your boon
if you obey them,
they will work your weal
if you win them:
be never the first
with friend of thine
to break the bond of fellowship;
care shall gnaw your heart
if you cannot tell
all your mind to another.

122. I counsel you, Stray-Singer,
accept my counsels,
they will be your boon
if you obey them,
they will work your weal
if you win them:
never in speech
with a foolish knave
should you waste a single word.

123. From the lips of such
you need not look
for reward of thine
own good will;
but a righteous man by praise
will render you firm
in favour and love.
124. There is mingling in friendship
when man can utter
all his whole mind to another;
there is nothing so vile
as a fickle tongue;
no friend is he who but flatters.

125. I counsel you, Stray-Singer,
accept my counsels,
they will be your boon
if you obey them,
they will work your weal
if you win them:
often the worst
lays the best one low.

126. I counsel you, Stray-Singer,
accept my counsels,
they will be your boon
if you obey them,
they will work your weal
if you win them:
be not a shoemaker
nor yet a shaft maker
save for yourself alone:
let the shoe be misshapen,
or crooked the shaft,
and a curse on your head
will be called.

127. I counsel you, Stray-Singer,
accept my counsels,
they will be your boon
if you obey them,
they will work your weal
if you win them:
when in peril you see you,
confess you in peril,
nor ever give peace to your foes.

128. I counsel you, Stray-Singer,
accept my counsels,
they will be your boon
if you obey them,
they will work your
weal if you win them:
rejoice not ever at tidings of ill,
but glad let your soul be in good.

129. I counsel you, Stray-Singer,
accept my counsels,
they will be your boon
if you obey them,
they will work your weal
if you win them:
look not up in battle,
when men are as beasts,
lest the wights
bewitch you with spells.

130. I counsel you, Stray-Singer,
accept my counsels,
they will be your boon
if you obey them,
they will work your weal
if you win them:
would you win joy
of a gentle maiden,
and lure to whispering of love,
make fair promise,
and let it be fast, -
none will scorn their weal
who can win it.

131. I counsel you, Stray-Singer,
accept my counsels,
they will be your boon
if you obey them,
they will work your weal
if you win them:
I pray you be wary,
yet not too wary,
be wariest of all with ale,
with another's wife,
and a third thing eke,
that knaves outwit you never.

132. I counsel you, Stray-Singer,
accept my counsels,
they will be your boon
if you obey them,
they will work your weal
if you win them:
hold not in scorn,
nor mock in your halls
a guest or wandering wight.

133. They know but unsurely
who sit within
what kind of man is come:
none is found so good,
but some fault attends him,
or so ill
but he serves for somewhat.

134. I counsel you, Stray-Singer,
accept my counsels,
they will be your boon
if you obey them,
they will work your weal
if you win them:
hold never in scorn
the hoary singer;
often the counsel
of the old is good;
come words of wisdom
from the withered lips
of him left to hang among hides,
to rock with the rennets.

135. I counsel you, Stray-Singer,
accept my counsels,
they will be your boon
if you obey them,
they will work your weal
if you win them:
growl not at guests,
nor drive them from the gate
but show yourself
gentle to the poor.

136. Mighty is the bar
to be moved away
for the entering in of all.
Shower your wealth,
or men shall wish you
every ill in your limbs.

137. I counsel you, Stray-Singer,
accept my counsels,
they will be your boon
if you obey them,
they will work your weal
if you win them:
when ale you quaffest,
call upon earth's might –
it is earth drinks in the floods.
Earth prevails over drink,
but fire over sickness, the oak over binding, the
earcorn over witchcraft, the rye spur over
rupture, the moon over rages.

The Hávamál

Part 4 - The Rune Poem (138-146)

138. I trow I hung on that windy Tree
nine whole days and nights,
stabbed with a spear,
offered to Óðinn,
myself to mine own self given,
high on that Tree
of which none has heard
from what roots it rises to heaven.

139. None refreshed me ever
with food or drink,
I peered right down in the deep;
crying aloud I lifted the Runes
then back I fell from thence.

140. Nine mighty songs
I learned from the great son
of Bale-thorn, Bestla's sire;
I drank a measure
of the wondrous Mead,
with the Soulstirrer's drops
I was showered.

141. Before long I bare fruit,
and throve full well,
I grew and waxed in wisdom;
word following word,
I found me words,
deed following deed,
I wrought deeds.

142. Hidden Runes shall you seek
and interpreted signs,
many symbols
of might and power,
by the great Singer painted,
by the high Powers fashioned,
graved by the Utterer of gods.

143. For gods graved Óðinn,
for elves graved Dan,
Dvalin the Dallier for dwarfs,
All-wise for Jotuns,
and I, of myself,
graved some for the sons of men.

144. Do you now how to write,
know how to read,
know how to paint,
know how to prove,
know how to ask,
know how to offer,
know how to send,
know how to spend?

145. Better ask for too little
than offer too much,
like the gift should be the boon;
better not to spend
than to overspend.
Thus Óðinn graved
before the world began;
Then he rose from the deep,
and came again.

The Hávamál

**Part 5 - Magic Charms
(146 - 164)**

146. Those songs I know,
which nor sons of men nor queen
in a king's court knows;
the first is Help
which will bring you help
in all woes and in sorrow and strife.

147. A second I know,
which the son of men must sing,
who would heal the sick.

148. A third I know:
if sore need should come
of a spell to stay my foes;
when I sing that song,
which shall blunt their swords,
nor their weapons
nor staves can wound.

149. A fourth I know:
if men make fast
in chains the joints of my limbs,
when I sing that song
which shall set me free,
spring the fetters
from hands and feet.

150. A fifth I know:
when I see, by foes shot,
speeding a shaft through the host,
flies it never so strongly
I still can stay it,
if I get but a glimpse of its flight.

151. A sixth I know:
when some thane
would harm me
in runes on a moist tree's root,
on his head alone
shall light the ills
of the curse
that he called upon mine.

152. A seventh I know:
if I see a hall high over
the bench-mates blazing,
flame it never so fiercely
I still can save it, -
I know how to sing that song.

153. An eighth I know:
which all can sing
for their weal
if they learn it well;
where hate shall wax
'mid the warrior sons,
I can calm it soon with that song.

154. A ninth I know:
when need befalls me
to save my vessel afloat,
I hush the wind
on the stormy wave,
and soothe all the sea to rest.

155. A tenth I know:
when at night the witches
ride and sport in the air,
such spells I weave
that they wander home
out of skins and wits bewildered.

156. An eleventh I know:
if haply I lead
my old comrades out to war,
I sing 'neath the shields,
and they fare forth mightily
safe into battle,
safe out of battle,
and safe return from the strife.

157. A twelfth I know:
if I see in a tree
a corpse from a halter hanging,
such spells I write,
and paint in runes,
that the being descends
and speaks.

158. A thirteenth I know:
if the new-born son of a warrior
I sprinkle with water,
that youth will not fail
when he fares to war,
never slain
shall he bow before sword.

159. A fourteenth I know:
if I needs must number
the Powers to the people of men,
I know all the nature
of gods and of elves
which none can know untaught.

160. A fifteenth I know,
which Folk-stirrer sang,
the dwarf, at the gates of Dawn;
he sang strength to the gods,
and skill to the elves,
and wisdom to Óðinn who utters.

161. A sixteenth I know:
when all sweetness and love
I would win
from some artful wench,
her heart I turn,
and the whole mind change
of that fair-armed lady I love.

162. A seventeenth I know:
so that even the shy maiden
is slow to shun my love.

These songs, Stray-Singer,
which man's son knows not,
long shall you lack in life,
though your weal
if you win them,
your boon if you obey them
your good if haply you gain them.

163. An eighteenth I know:
which I never shall tell
to maiden or wife of man
save alone to my sister,
or haply to her
who folds me fast in her arms;
most safe are secrets
known to but one-
the songs are sung to an end.

164. Now the sayings of the High One
are uttered in the hall
for the weal of men,
for the woe of Jotuns,
Hail, you who have spoken!
Hail, you that knowest!
Hail, you that have hearkened!
Use, you who have learned!